cloverleaf books™

Fall's Here!

Fall Weather
Cooler Temperatures

Martha E. H. Rustad
illustrated by **Amanda Enright**

M MILLBROOK PRESS · MINNEAPOLIS

For Melissa, who loves fall weather
and fall camping —M. E. H. R.

Millbrook Press
A division of Lerner Publishing Group, Inc.
241 First Avenue North
Minneapolis, MN 55401 U.S.A.

Website address: www.lernerbooks.com

Main body text set in Slappy Inline 18/28.
Typeface provided by T26.

Library of Congress Cataloging-in-Publication Data

Rustad, Martha E. H. (Martha Elizabeth Hillman), 1975–
    Fall Weather : Cooler Temperatures / by Martha E. H.
Rustad ; illustrated by Amanda Enright.
        p.   cm. (Cloverleaf Books™—Fall's Here!)
    Includes index.
    ISBN: 978-0-7613-5063-7 (lib. bdg. : alk. paper)
    1. Autumn—Juvenile literature. I. Enright, Amanda, ill.
II. Title.
QB637.7R868 2012
508.2—dc22   2010048309

Manufactured in the United States of America
1 – BP – 7/15/11

TABLE OF CONTENTS

Chapter One

Fall Begins

Whoosh!
Wind blows colorful leaves across the yard.
Fall weather is here.

We grab our jackets. We go outside to rake. We jump onto the leaf pile, and the leaves fly up.

Fall and autumn are names for the same season. People call the season fall because leaves fall from trees this time of year.

Today our class celebrates the **first day of fall**. Every year, fall begins on September 22 or 23. People call this day the **fall equinox**.

On the equinox, day and night are the same length. Day lasts about twelve hours. Night lasts about twelve hours too.

The word *equinox* means "equal night."

During fall, each day is a **little shorter** than the day before.

Fall ends on December 21 or 22. We call the first day of winter the winter solstice. It is the shortest day and longest night of the year.

Every morning, **the sun rises later.**

Every night, the **sun sets earlier.**
Less daylight brings cooler weather.

Chapter Two
Changing Weather

Throughout fall, we feel the weather change from **warm to cold**.
Our part of the planet gets the most sunlight during summer.

It gets the least sunlight during winter.
Fall weather feels cooler than summer weather.
Fall weather feels warmer than winter weather.

Animals notice cooler weather too. They get ready for winter during fall. Some animals grow thicker coats of fur. Others hide food so they can eat it later.

Fall weather changes from day to day.
We **check the weather** each morning to decide what to wear.

Meteorologists are scientists. They study weather and predict the weather each day.

In September, we wear light jackets. In October, we may put on hats. By November, we might need warm coats and mittens.

Chapter Three

Weather Chart

Our class is making a weather chart this fall. Every day, we look at the rain gauge.

We write down how much rain fell.
Every day, we look at the thermometer.
We write down the temperature.

day	date	rain gauge	temp
Monday	11/2	2.5 in. (6 cm)	50°F (10°C)
Tuesday	11/3	1 in. (3 cm)	48°F (9°C)
Wednesday	11/4	3 in. (8 cm)	39°F (4°C)
Thursday	11/5	0 in. (0 cm)	43°F (6°C)
Friday	11/6	0 in. (0 cm)	35°F (2°C)
Monday	11/9	1 in. (3 cm)	34°F (2°C)
	11/10	1 in. (3 cm)	34°F (2°C)

Some places have a rainy season during fall. People in these places carry umbrellas or wear rain jackets nearly every day.

Some days, we write down warm temperatures.
Some days, we write down cool temperatures.

As the weeks pass, we make an observation.

The temperature is going down.

An observation is something you see or learn after carefully studying something else.

We compare our chart with charts
from classes in other places.

One class has **warmer weather.**

Another class has **more rain.**

My class has **snow** in the fall.

Fall weather is different from place to place.

Some parts of Earth do not have fall weather. The weather around the middle of Earth is nearly the same all year.

19

Chapter Four
Fall Ends

Fall is **nearly over** now.
We wear heavy coats to stay warm outside.

We see frost on the grass some mornings.
Soon snowflakes fly through the air.
Winter is almost here.

Make a Rain Gauge

A rain gauge is a tool that records rainfall. **Ask an adult to help with this craft.**

Equipment:
clear drinking straw
ruler
fine-tip marker
empty container with a flat bottom (such as an empty coffee can or soup can)

1) Lay the plastic drinking straw flat on a table. Line up the ruler with the bottom. Mark ¼ inches, ½ inches, ¾ inches, 1 inch, 1¼ inches, etc.

2) Set your container in an open place outside. Find a place that is far away from buildings or trees that could affect how much rain can fall into it. Make sure your container rests on an even surface.

3) To measure rainfall, put the straw (small numbers down) into the container. Be sure to touch the bottom. Put your finger on top to hold the water in. Pull the straw out. Record how much rain is in it.

GLOSSARY

autumn: the season between summer and winter. This season is also often called fall.

equinox: the date when day and night are each twelve hours long. The spring equinox is March 19 or 20, and the fall equinox is September 22 or 23.

observation: something you can see or learn when you study something carefully

rain gauge: a tool that catches and measures the amount of precipitation that falls

temperature: how hot or cold something is

thermometer: a tool that measures how hot or cold something is

BOOKS

Anderson, Sheila. *Are You Ready for Fall?* Minneapolis: Lerner Publications Company, 2010.

Rustad, Martha. *Fall Leaves.* Minneapolis: Millbrook Press, 2011.

Sterling, Kristin. *It's Rainy Today.* Minneapolis: Lerner Publications Company, 2010.

WEBSITES

Brain Pop Jr.
http://www.brainpopjr.com/science/weather/
Watch short movies that explain changes in the weather.

Enchanted Learning: Fall (Autumn) Crafts
http://www.enchantedlearning.com/crafts/fall/
Celebrate the fall season with this site's cool activities and coloring pages.

National Geographic Kids: Weather Word Search
http://kids.nationalgeographic.com/kids/games/puzzlesquizzes/weather-word-search/
Check out this fun word search, and see how many weather words you can find.